REAL LIVES

Coventry City

Michael Keane

Published in association with The Basic Skills Agency

Hodder & Stoughton

A MEMBER OF THE HODDER HEADLINE GROUP

Acknowledgements
Cover: Jamie McDonald/Allsport

Photos: pp iv, 10 © Coventry Evening Telegraph; p 2 © John Walton/Empics; p 19, 24 © Allsport; p 21 © Peter Robinson/Empics.

Every effort has been made to trace copyright holders of material reproduced in this book. Any rights not acknowledged will be acknowledged in subsequent printings if notice is given to the publisher.

Orders; please contact Bookpoint Ltd, 39 Milton Park, Abingdon, Oxon OX14 4TD. Telephone (44) 01235 400414, Fax: (44) 01235 400454. Lines are open from 9.00–6.00, Monday to Saturday, with a 24 hour message answering service.
Email address: orders@bookpoint.co.uk

British Library Cataloguing in Publication Data
A catalogue record for this title is available from the British Library

ISBN 0 340 80097 6

First published 2001
Impression number 10 9 8 7 6 5 4 3 2 1
Year 2007 2006 2005 2004 2003 2002 2001

Typeset by SX Composing DTP, Rayleigh, Essex
Printed in Great Britain for Hodder & Stoughton Educational, a division of Hodder Headline Plc, 338 Euston Road, London NW1 3BH by Redwood Books, Trowbridge, Wilts.

Contents

Workers at the Singers Cycle factory set up Singers FC. In 1898 they changed their name to Coventry City FC.

1 Beginnings

In 1883, a cycle firm in Coventry
started a football team.
The team was founded in a pub.
The cycle firm was called Singers.
Their team was called Singers FC.
That team became Coventry City,
the same Coventry City
which now plays in the Premier League.

In 1898, Singers FC changed their name.
They changed it to Coventry City,
because they played in Coventry.

In 1899, Coventry City moved to Highfield Road.
Coventry City have played at Highfield Road
ever since.
In fact, they have played there for over 100 years.

Coventry City have played at Highfield since 1899.

2 Early Days

1919 was a very important year for Coventry City.
It was the year Coventry
joined the Football League.
They started in Division Two.
They have played in the League ever since.

Coventry City lost their first ever game in
the Football League.
Totttenham beat them 5–0 at Highfield Road!
For a long time, things did not get much better.
Coventry played eleven games
and did not score in any of them.
This terrible run is still a record for Coventry City.
Coventry did not win any games
until Christmas Day 1919.

On the last day of the season
Coventry just escaped being relegated.
This has happened lots of times since!

So, in the early years, Coventry did not do well.
They were always near the bottom of Division Two.
Coventry were finally relegated in 1925.

It took eleven years
to be promoted back to Division Two.
The team was much stronger then.
The team had one real star player.
The star player was called Clarrie Bourton.

Bourton scored 49 goals in one season.
No Coventry player has ever scored
that many goals in a season since.
Bourton scored 181 goals for Coventry
in the 1930s.

Nobody else has ever scored
that many goals for Coventry since.
Not even Dion Dublin!
Clarrie Bourton is still the club's
record goal-scorer.

Clarrie Bourton is Coventry City's
record goal-scorer.

3 Ups and Downs

The 1950s were a very bad time for Coventry.
The team dropped from Division Two
to Division Three again.
Then they dropped from Division Three
to Division Four.
Things were getting worse and worse for Coventry.

In 1959 Coventry came second in Division Four.
At last, things were getting better.

A new manager arrived in 1961,
he was called Jimmy Hill.
You might have seen Jimmy Hill on television.
Now he is a famous commentator.
In the 1960s, Jimmy Hill was
a great football manager.
He helped Coventry
climb up the football ladder again.

4 The Sky Blues

Lots of things changed for Coventry in the 1960s.
Jimmy Hill changed the team's colours
from all white to sky blue.
The club's nickname changed to 'The Sky Blues'.
Even Highfield Road changed.
Bigger and better stands were built.
The best change was on the pitch
– City started to win!

Coventry had some star players.
Bobby Gould was a strong striker,
who scored lots of goals.
George Curtis was a tough defender.
His nickname was the 'Iron Man',
because he was so strong.

Coventry got better and better.
In 1964, the Sky Blues were champions of
Division Three.
In 1966, the Sky blues came third in Division Two.
They missed promotion by one point.
The Sky Blues were getting closer and closer
to their dream.
Their dream was to play in the First Division.

Jimmy Hill helped Coventry City to reach Division One.

The 1967 season was another good one for the Sky Blues.
By April, they were second in Division Two.
Wolves were the only team ahead of them.
The next game was Coventry against Wolves, at Highfield Road.

Some people called this game the 'Midlands' Match of the Century'.
It seemed that everyone wanted to watch.
People climbed onto the roof of the stand, to get a good view.
People climbed up the floodlights, to get a good view.
The ground was fuller than it had ever been.

Over 50,000 people watched.
Wolves scored first and were winning 1–0 at half-time.
But three second-half goals gave the Sky Blues a brilliant 3–1 win.
Two weeks later Coventry were champions of Division Two.

Coventry were going to play in the First Division.
At last, all their dreams had come true.

People even climbed up the floodlights to watch the 'Midlands' Match of the Century'.

5 The First Division

When Coventry were promoted,
people thought they would struggle.
Those people were right!
Coventry found the First Division hard.

For the first two years, they just escaped relegation.
The next year Coventry came sixth.
They have never finished so high since.

In 1970, the Sky Blues played in Europe.
First, they beat a team from Bulgaria.
Then they had to play Bayern Munich,
from Germany, at home and in Germany.
Coventry beat Munich 2–1 at Highfield Road.
The bad news was Munich had won
the first game 6–1.

The Sky Blues have not played in Europe since.

Coventry have played in the top division
for over thirty years.
In thirty years, they have never been relegated.
But they have come close to relegation lots of times!
Coventry City are good at escaping.

People say Coventry are like Harry Houdini.
He could escape from anything.
He used to be tied up in knots and chains.
Then he would have to escape.

Harry Houdini always escaped at the last minute.
And Coventry City have always escaped
at the last minute too.

Ten times in thirty years,
Coventry have played their last
match of the season,
still worrying about relegation.
Ten times in thirty years,
Coventry have escaped on the last day.

In the 1970s, the Sky Blues' highest place
in the League was seventh.
Most years they were in the bottom half.

In the 1980s, things were just as bad.
New managers came.
New players came.
But Coventry were always near the bottom.
There were some great escapes.
One of the best escapes was in 1985.

In 1985, the Sky Blues had to win
all of their last three matches.
First, they beat Stoke 1–0, with a penalty.
Then they played Luton Town.
With twenty minutes left, it was 0–0.
With ten minutes left, it was 0–0.
Everyone thought Coventry must be relegated.
With only five minutes left, Coventry scored.

Coventry thrashed the champions Everton 4–1
in the last game of three.

It was another great escape.
Even Harry Houdini would have been proud
of that one.

6 'We're Going to Wembley . . .'

The Sky Blues kicked off the 1986–87 season
with two managers in charge, instead of one.
George Curtis and John Sillett
had both played for the club.
They had both played in the 1960s.
They had both played
when Coventry were winning.

The two managers soon got the team playing well.
The Sky Blues did not lose many matches;
they were very hard to beat.
At Highfield Road
the Sky Blues won most of their matches.
People said this was the best Coventry
team for years.

By Christmas,
Coventry were in the top half of the League.
At last, the Sky Blues were having a good year.
Some people did not think
the Sky Blues could play well all season.
Those people were soon proved wrong.

In the FA Cup, Coventry beat Bolton easily.
The next match was much harder;
it was away at Manchester United.
It was going to be a very hard game for the Sky Blues.

In the first half,
Keith Houchen scored for the Sky Blues.
After that, United had lots of the play.
The Coventry defenders had an excellent game.
United just could not score.
There were no more goals.
United were out and the Sky Blues were through.

In the next round, Coventry beat Stoke City 1–0.
This was another touch match,
but it was another win.
Suddenly, Coventry City were in the quarter-finals of the FA Cup.
In 104 years, the Sky Blues had never got past this round.

In the quarter-final,
the Sky Blues had to play away again.
They played Sheffield Wednesday, at Hillsborough.
Nearly 50,000 noisy fans watched.

The home fans went quiet when Regis
scored a great goal.
After an hour Wednesday made it 1–1.
City's dreams of winning the cup
were staring to fade away.
They needed something special.

Striker Keith Houchen was about to be taken off.
He got the ball in the Sheffield half.
He ran and ran with it.
There was no Coventry player near him,
so he tried a shot.
The ball was deflected.
It flew into the goal for 2–1.
Five minutes later, Houchen scored another.
After that, no-one dared take him off.

Coventry City were in the FA Cup semi-final.
Wembley was only one game away.

Coventry played Leeds United in the semi-final.
It was the biggest match City had played for years.
The game was played in Sheffield again,
at Hillsborough.
The winners would go to Wembley.

Leeds were in the Second Division at the time.
Everyone thought
Coventry would be able to beat them easily.
It was anything but easy.

For a long time Leeds were winning 1–0.
Coventry's goalie, Steve Ogrizovic,
had to make some brilliant saves.
At full-time the score was 2–2.
The teams had to play extra-time.
Both teams were very tired,
but Coventry kept on attacking.
Dave Bennett finally scored
the winning goal for Coventry.
It was the goal that sent the Sky Blues to Wembley.

The fans were singing 'We're going to Wembley'.
For the first time in 104 years, they were right.

7 The 1987 FA Cup Final

At long last Coventry City were in the FA Cup Final.
The whole city of Coventry
was talking about the game.
Everyone wanted tickets for the match.
Everyone wanted the Sky Blues to win.

Tottenham were the team City had to beat.
At Christmas, Coventry had beaten
Tottenham 4–3 in a great match.
Could they do it again?

Wembley stadium was full of noise and colour.
The Sky Blues' fans were having a great day out.
Everyone was ready for a terrific game.
Everyone was ready, apart from
the Coventry defence.
After only sixty seconds Tottenham scored!
It was a terrible start.

After ten minutes though, Coventry were level.
Dave Bennett darted past the
Tottenham defence to score.
It looked like it was going to be a fantastic final.

Keith Houchen scored with a brilliant header against Tottenham.

The game twisted and turned.
Tottenham had good spells,
then Coventry had good spells.
Tottenham scored a second goal.
Coventry scored a second goal.

Coventry's second goal
was one of the best ever seen at Wembley.
Keith Houchen dived a long way
to head the ball in.
It was a brilliant goal.

As the game went on
Tottenham had less of the ball.
Coventry had more of the shots.
Coventry had become the stronger team.

In extra-time the winning goal was scored.
Coventry's Lloyd McGrath crossed the ball.
It hit Tottenham player Gary Mabbutt's knee.
The ball looped up high.
It went over the Tottenham goalie into the net.
Coventry had won 3–2.

After 104 years, the cup was going to Coventry!

After 104 years, Coventry finally won the FA Cup.

8 The Premier League

Coventry City play in the Premier League now.
Some fans say the Premier League
is the most exciting league in the world.
The Premier League has some of the best players,
and best teams, in the world.

The Sky Blues have played in the Premier League
since it started in 1992.
So far, Coventry have never finished in the top ten.
They have had some hard years.
And of course, they have battled against relegation.

In 1997, they had to win their last match to be safe.
It was a hard last match, away at Tottenham.
Coventry have played some great matches
against Tottenham.
This one was another.
The Sky Blues won 2–1.
None of the other teams near the bottom
won their last games.
Coventry were safe again.

Coventry have not yet had a great team
in the Premier League.
But they have had some great players.
Exciting players like
Dion Dublin and Robbie Keane
have been stars for Coventry.

Dion Dublin scored lots of goals.
He is a great centre-forward.
He even played for England.

Robbie Keane was a fast and tricky player.
He could go past defenders easily.
He scored some brilliant goals.

Dublin and Keane were very popular players,
but they have left.
Sky Blues fans are now looking
for new heroes to cheer on.

Dion Dublin scored lots of goals for Coventry City.

Coventry are making some big changes in the future.
They are going to leave Highfield Road.
They are building a new ground.
It will open in the next couple of years.

The new stadium will hold 40,000 people.
It will have a roof on it.
And the pitch will be rolled away
when it is not being used!
The new stadium will be one of the best
in the country.

Coventry have come a long, long way
since the days of Singers FC.
In the new century,
we will see how much further they can go.
Sky Blues' fans hope there are exciting times ahead.

9 Did You Know?

Coventry have had some great wins over the years.
They once won a match 9–0 against
Bristol City in 1934.

Lots of records were set in the 1930s.
coventry's record goal scorer, Clarrie Bourton,
scored 181 goals in the 1930s.

In 1932, Coventry scored over 100 goals.
They did that again in 1933, 1934
and 1936!

Football has changed since then.
Now, it is harder to score goals.
Defences have got a lot better!

Big scores do not happen very often.
Coventry's biggest win for 30 years
came in 1999.

Macclesfield Town came to play in the FA Cup.
Coventry played brilliantly.
They could not stop scoring.
It ended up 7–0 to the Sky Blues.

Games like that are talked about
for a very long time.

Coventry fans wish they could score
so many goals now.
Because scoring goals is what
makes football so exciting.

League History

Coventry City have had lots of ups and downs!

1894 to 1908 Birmingham and District League
1908 to 1915 Southern League
1919 to 1925 Football League Division 2
1925 to 1936 Football League Division 3
1936 to 1952 Football League Division 2
1952 to 1958 Football League Division 3
1958 to 1959 Football League Division 4
1959 to 1964 Football League Division 3
1964 to 1967 Football League Division 2
1967 to 1992 Football League Division 1
1992 to present FA Carling Premiership